WARSHIP PICTORIAL #26

Kriegsmarine Tir

by John Asmussen & Steve Wiper

Illustrations by John Asmussen & Steve Wiper

Tirpitz *during sea trials in the Baltic Sea, summer 1941. The top and slopes of the main turrets, as well as the barrels of the guns were painted black at that time.*

CLASSIC WARSHIPS PUBLISHING

P. O. Box 57591 • Tucson, AZ. 85732 • USA
Web Site: www.classicwarships.com • Ph/Fx (520)748-2992
Copyright © January 2005
ISBN 0-9745687-5-9
Printed by Arizona Lithographers, Tucson, Arizona

General History of the German Battleship *Tirpitz*

14 June 1936: The building contract was placed with the Kriegsmarine Werft Shipyard, Wilhelmshaven, Germany, as battleship "G". It was construction number 128 at the Shipyard and it took place on Slipway 2.

2 November 1936: Keel was laid down.

1 April 1939: *Tirpitz* launched. Christened by Frau von Hassel, daughter of Grand Admiral Tirpitz, after whom the ship was named.

9-10 July 1940: That night, the first specific attack against *Tirpitz* involved 11 British "5 Group" Hampdens. *Tirpitz* was still under construction at the Kriegsmarine Werft, Wilhelmshaven. Target was missed.

20-21 July 1940: Another night raid, 15 Hampdens from 61 and 144 Squadron took off from Hemswell-Lincolnshire to attack the heavy cruiser, *Admiral Scheer*, and *Tirpitz* in Wilhelmshaven. The aircraft used mines with soluble fuse and they managed to hit the inner harbor of Wilhelmshaven. The mines exploded after 40 minutes without damaging the ships.

24-25 July 1940: At night, 14 "4 Group" Whitleys went off to attack *Tirpitz* at Wilhelmshaven. Only two of the planes actually reached the area at Wilhelmshaven. Bad weather conditions forced the other twelve aircraft to abort the operation. The British again failed to hit *Tirpitz*.

5-6 October 1940: Another inconclusive attack by "5 Group" Hampdens.

8-9 October 1940: Night raid by 17 aircraft attacked *Tirpitz* at Wilhelmshaven. No hits scored. The aircraft came from airfields in Scampton and Waddington (Lincolnshire).

10-11 October 1940: Fourteen aircraft made another night attack against *Tirpitz*. No direct hits. The aircraft came from airfields in Waddington (Lincolnshire) and Lindholme (Yorkshire).

12-13 October 1940: At night, 40 "3 Group" Wellingtons and 35 "5 Group" Hampdens set out for *Scharnhorst* and *Gneisenau* in Kiel and *Tirpitz* in Wilhelmshaven. Due to bad weather only 4 Hampdens even located Wilhelmshaven. No hits were scored.

19-20 October 1940: Night raid by 7 "3 Group" Wellingtons attacked *Tirpitz* in Wilhelmshaven. No

direct hits were reported on the battleship.

25-26 November 1940: Five "4 Group" aircraft from 51 and 78 Squadrons attacked at night during bad weather conditions. Again no hits were scored.

8-9 January 1941: Seven Wellingtons of 75 Squadron from Feltwell (Lincolnshire) attacked *Tirpitz* at Wilhelmshaven in another night raid. Some hits or near misses were claimed.

11-12 January 1941: At night, 16 aircraft from 49 and 83 Squadrons took off from Scampton (Lincolnshire) to attack *Tirpitz*, which was still at the builders yard at Wilhelmshaven. No hits were scored.

16-17 January 1941: Eight Hampdens from 83 Squadron took off to attack *Tirpitz*. Bad weather caused two aircraft to return early and one to ditch in North Sea with engine trouble. Only two of eight aircraft from Waddington (Lincolnshire) attacked, with no success.

29-30 January 1941: Night raid by 25 "3 Group" Wellingtons flew to bomb *Tirpitz*. All aircraft reached the Wilhelmshaven area, but no bombs hit *Tirpitz*.

9 February 1941: 13 aircraft of 83 Squadron from Scampton (Lincolnshire) took off for Wilhelmshaven to attack *Tirpitz*. They failed to hit the battleship.

25 February 1941: *Tirpitz* was commissioned and placed under the command of Kapitän zur See (Captain) Friedrich Karl Topp.

27-28 February 1941: A night raid by 30 Wellingtons from 40, 115, 214 and 218 Squadrons based at Wyton (Cambridgeshire), Marham (Norfolk) and Stradishall (Suffolk) took off to attack *Tirpitz*. 26 of the 30 aircraft attacked, but weather interfered greatly with the success of the operation, with no reliable observation of hits.

28 February-1 March 1941: At night, 23 "5 Group" aircraft left Scampton and Waddington (Lincolnshire) to attack *Tirpitz*. Cloud level down to 2700 meters (9000 feet) in target area, coupled with ground haze made identification impossible. 4 aircraft bombed position of ship without any success.

9 March 1941: *Tirpitz* left Wilhelmshaven for the first time and anchored at the Jade outside Wilhelmshaven.

11 March 1941: *Tirpitz* departed for Kiel through the

river Elbe and Kaiser Wilhelm Kanal.

12 March 1941: *Tirpitz* arrived in Kiel and anchored at Strander Bucht at the Kieler Förde.

13 March 1941: *Tirpitz* raised anchor and headed for Gotenhafen, Poland where it arrived next day.

20 March 1941: Left Gotenhafen to conduct trials in the Danziger Bucht and the eastern part of the Baltic Sea.

Early May 1941: *Tirpitz* returned to Gotenhafen.

5 May 1941: Adolf Hitler visited naval yard at Gotenhafen, inspecting both *Tirpitz* and *Bismarck*, which were anchored in the roadstead. After the visit, *Bismarck* departed for Norway and *Tirpitz* continued her trials in Baltic Sea.

13 June 1941: *Tirpitz* arrived to Deutsche Werke shipyard in Kiel to have remaining work on ship completed.

7 September 1941: Work on the ship completed.

11 September 1941: Continued trials in the Baltic Sea.

23-26 September 1941: Member of the so-called "Baltic Fleet". While still on trials, *Tirpitz* joined a powerful assembly of German warships off the Aaland Islands to deter the Soviet fleet from venturing out of Kronstadt. The "Baltic Fleet" consisted of *Tirpitz*, *Admiral Scheer*, *Emden*, *Leipzig*, *Köln* and *Nürnberg*, together with numerous destroyers, torpedo boats and mine sweepers. After that, *Tirpitz* continued her trials.

29 December 1941: The decision of sending *Tirpitz* to Norway was made. The loss of *Bismarck* forced the Germans to think carefully about *Tirpitz*. It was decided to transfer the battleship to Norway because as Grand Admiral Erich Raeder said: "to protect our position in the Norwegian and Arctic areas by threatening the flank of enemy operations against the northern Norwegian areas, and by attacking White Sea convoys to tie down enemy forces in the Atlantic, so that they cannot operate in the Mediterranean, Indian or Pacific Oceans."

6 January 1942: Grand Admiral Erich Raeder inspected *Tirpitz* at Gotenhafen.

10 January 1942: *Tirpitz* declared fully operational.

11 January 1942: *Tirpitz* prepared for Operation "Polarnacht", the transfer of the ship from Germany to Norway. *Tirpitz* slowly started to head for the Jade outside

Wilhelmshaven. On its way it carried out further trials.

14 January 1942: 1430 hrs., *Tirpitz* anchored in the Jade outside Wilhelmshaven.

14 January 1942: 2350 hrs., *Tirpitz*, escorted by destroyers *Richard Beitzen*, *Paul Jacobi*, *Bruno Heinemann* and *Z-29*, transferred from Wilhelmshaven, Germany to Trondheim, Norway, four days later than originally planned.

16 January 1942: *Tirpitz* arrived, together with the destroyers, at Trondheim in Norway and anchored in Faettenfjord at 1745 hrs., protected by torpedo nets.

30 January 1942: Operation Oiled, first British attempt to attack *Tirpitz* in Norway. Seven Short Stirlings of 15 and 149 Squadrons took of from Lossiemouth at 0030 hrs. and 9 Halifaxes of 10 and 76 Squadrons took off from Lossiemouth between 0204 and 0234 hrs. Due to bad weather the aircraft were not able to attack.

6-9 March 1942: Operation Sportpalast, first combat action against Allied convoys by *Tirpitz*, which sailed, in company with the destroyers *Z-25*, *Friedrich Ihn* and *Hermann Schoemann*, into the Arctic Ocean to intercept the convoys PQ-12 and QP-8. Due to bad weather the German battle group failed to contact the enemy convoys. *Tirpitz* sailed to the Lofoten islands and anchored in Bogen near Narvik.

9 March 1942: On her way to the Lofoten islands, *Tirpitz* was attacked by 12 Albacores from the British aircraft carrier *Victorious*. The attack failed and 2 Albacores were shot down.

12 March 1942: *Tirpitz* left Bogen and headed back to Faettenfjord near Trondheim.

13 March 1942: *Tirpitz* arrived at Faettenfjord.

30-31 March 1942: *Tirpitz* was attacked during the night by 32 Halifaxes from 10 Squadron (10 aircraft took of from Lossiemouth, Scotland), 35 Squadron (12 aircraft took off from Kinloss, Scotland) and 76 Squadron (10 aircraft took off from Tain, Scotland). The attack was unsuccessful due to bad weather.

27-28 April 1942: *Tirpitz* attacked, at night, by 30 Halifax bombers from 10, 35 and 76 Squadrons and 11 Lancasters from 44 and 97 Squadrons. The attack was unsuccessful.

28-29 April 1942: At night, *Tirpitz* was attacked by 21 Halifax bombers from 10, 35 and 76 Squadrons and 12 Lancasters from 44 and 97 Squadrons.

2-4 July 1942: Operation Musik, transfer of *Tirpitz*, *Admiral Hipper*, *Friedrich Ihn*, *Hans Lody*, *Karl Galster*, *Theodor Riedel*, *T-7* and *T-15* from Trondheim to Alta via Bogen. This was in preparation for an attack against Russian bound Allied convoy PQ-17.

5-6 July 1942: Operation Rösselsprung, together with 16 other ships, divided in two battle groups, *Tirpitz* participated in an attack against convoy PQ-17. The two battle groups consisted of; Battle Group I: Under Fleet Commander, Admiral Schniewind on board *Tirpitz*, consisted of *Tirpitz*, *Admiral Hipper*, *Friedrich Ihn*, *Hans Lody*, *Karl Galster*, *Theodor Riedel*, *Richard Beitzen*, *T-7* and *T-15*. Battle Group II: Under Vice-Admiral Kummetz on board *Lützow*, consisted of *Lützow*, *Admiral Scheer*, *Z-24*, *Z-27*, *Z-28*, *Z-29*, *Z-30* and the fleet oiler *Dithmarschen*.

5 July 1942: Late at night, the operation against convoy PQ-17 was cancelled after the breakdown of several supporting units and because the convoy already had been successfully attacked by aircraft and submarines. *Tirpitz* and escort was redrawn to Kaafjord near Alta.

6 July 1942: Arrived at 1040 hrs, refueled, with *Tirpitz*, *Admiral Scheer*, *Admiral Hipper*, destroyers *Friedrich Ihn*, *Richard Beitzen*, *Z-24*, *Z-27*, *Z-28*, *Z-29*, *Z-30* and torpedo boats *T-7*, *T-15* as well as tanker *Dithmarschen* left Kaafjord and headed for Bogen.

8 July 1942: Arrived at Bogen.

July 1942-October 1942: Several trials in Ofotfjord and Vestjord near Bogen.

23 October 1942: *Tirpitz* departed Bogen to be refitted in Faettenfjord/Lofjord near Trondheim, where necessary technical personnel were available.

24 October 1942: *Tirpitz* arrived in Faettenfjord.

30-31 October 1942: Operation Title, attempt by British to put *Tirpitz* out of action by using human torpedoes (Chariots). The mission was aborted when the Chariots broke away from the ship *Arthur* in Trondheimfjord. It was just about 16 kilometers away from *Tirpitz*.

18 November 1942: *Tirpitz* transferred from Faettenfjord to Lofjord to continue comprehensive work on the ship.

28 December 1942: Work on *Tirpitz* was completed.

January 1943-6 March 1943: *Tirpitz* carried out comprehensive trials and exercises in nearby waters.

11 March 1943: Operation Rostock, *Tirpitz*, in company with destroyers *Paul Jacobi*, *Karl Galster* and torpedo boats *Jaguar* and *Greif*, were transferred to Bogen.

13 March 1943: Arrived at 0100 hrs. Bogen. Here *Tirpitz* met up with *Scharnhorst* and *Lützow*.

22 March 1943: *Tirpitz*, *Scharnhorst*, *Lützow*, six destroyers and two torpedo boats left Bogen to sail to Kaafjord/Altenfjord.

24 March 1943: Arrived early morning.

April-Late August 1943: *Tirpitz* carried out trials and exercises together with *Scharnhorst*, *Lützow* and other smaller German units present.

6-9 September 1943: Operation Sizilien, squadron consisting of *Tirpitz*, *Scharnhorst* and destroyers *Erich Steinbrinck*, *Karl Galster*, *Hans Lody*, *Theodor Riedel*, *Z-27*, *Z-29*, *Z-30*, *Z-31*, and *Z-33*, went on to attack the Norwegian owned archipelago Spitsbergen. This was a vital location for Allied meteorologist's, whose reports had an important bearing on convoy operations.

8 September 1943: *Tirpitz* and *Scharnhorst* bombard and destroy Allied meteorological station.

9 September 1943: At 1730 hrs., *Tirpitz*, *Scharnhorst* and their escort returned safely to their bases in Kaafjord and Langfjord.

11 September 1943-5 October 1943: Operation Source, *Tirpitz* was attacked by British X-Craft midget submarines *X-5*, *X-6* and *X-7*. They broke through torpedo nets and *X-6* and *X-7* managed to place mines below the ship. All three midget submarines were lost.

23 September 1943: At 0812, the first charge from the *X-6* and *X-7* midget submarines exploded on the port side below *Tirpitz* about 6 m from the midship engine room followed shortly afterwards by a second explosion, 61 m abaft the port bow. The exploding mines caused severe damage on *Tirpitz*. Besides some hull damage, the turbines were put out of action, the propeller shafts and rudder were disabled. The casualties were, however, slight, with one dead and 40 wounded. *Tirpitz* was out of commission for the first time.

September 1943-March 1944: Repairs of damages caused by British X-Craft midget submarine attack took place in Kaafjord as it was considered too dangerous to transfer *Tirpitz* to Germany, due to risk of new attacks from British naval or air units. About 1000 shipyard workers were transferred to Kaajord on the ship *New York* and the repair ship *Neumark* was anchored next to *Tirpitz* during the repair period. The work was carried out under extremely difficult conditions.

10-11 February 1944: At night, 15 Russian bombers try to attack *Tirpitz* in Kaafjord. 11 bombers fail to find Kaafjord, but four aircraft locate Kaafjord and *Tirpitz* and they drop their 1,000 kg special bombs, with no hits.

15 March 1944: *Tirpitz* began trials in Barbrudalen (Kaafjord) and in Altenfjord.

3 April 1944: Operation Tungsten, *Tirpitz* attacked by 41 Barracudas from British aircraft carriers. The Germans admitted that 12 bombs hit the battleship, with 4 near misses. Damage to the ship was severe, with a high loss among the crew, 120 killed and 316 seriously wounded.

April 1944: Repair of the damages was started shortly after the attack.

24 April 1944: Operation Planet, from British aircraft carriers, attack *Tirpitz* with 40 Barracudas and 40 escort fighters, which had to be cancelled because of bad weather.

14 May 1944: *Tirpitz* was moved to a new location in Kaafjord where it would be anchored in the future.

15 May 1944: Operation Brawn, attack on *Tirpitz* from British aircraft carriers, involving 27 Barracudas and 36 escort fighters had to be cancelled due to bad weather.

28 May 1944: Operation Tiger Claw, attack on *Tirpitz* had to be cancelled before the aircraft could be launched, because of bad weather conditions.

21 June 1944: *Tirpitz* was ready for trials and exercises, which were carried out in Altenfjord.

17 July 1944: Operation Mascot, attack on *Tirpitz*, involving 44 Barracudas, 18 Hellcats and 30 escort fighters from British aircraft carriers *Formidable*, *Indefatigable* and *Furious*. *Tirpitz* had been forewarned and attacking aircraft were unable to hit the German battleship due to smoke screen.

31 July-1 August 1944: *Tirpitz* carried out exercises at sea for the last time, with the destroyers *Z-29*, *Z-31*, *Z-33*, *Z-34* and *Z-39*.

22 August 1944: Operation Goodwood I and II, *Tirpitz* was attacked by 32 Barracudas escorted by 43 fighters from the aircraft carriers *Formidable*, *Indefatigable*, *Furious*, *Nabob* and *Trumpeter*. *Tirpitz* received no hits.

24 August 1944: Operation Goodwood III, *Tirpitz* was attacked by 33 Barracudas, 10 Hellcats, 5 Corsairs and 29 fighters from the aircraft carriers *Indefatigable*, *Furious* and *Formidable*. 2 hits, one 226.8 kg and one 725.7 kg bomb, were scored with relatively little damage. Eight *Tirpitz* crew members killed and 13 wounded, at the cost of 2 British aircraft shot down.

29 August 1944: Operation Goodwood IV, *Tirpitz* was attacked by 26 Barracudas, 2 Corsairs, 3 Hellcats and 25 fighters from aircraft carriers *Formidable* and *Indefatigable*. No hits, several near misses, with 6 *Tirpitz* crew members wounded, again at the cost of 2 British aircraft shot down.

15 September 1944: Operation Paravane, *Tirpitz* attacked by 27 Lancasters from 9 and 617 Squadrons temporarily stationed in Yagodnik, USSR. Each Lancaster carried a single 5,443 ton "Tall Boy" bomb. Two of these bombs hit and penetrated the forecastle. The damage was very serious and *Tirpitz* was again out of action.

23 September 1944: Estimations that repairs of the damages would take at least 9 months, caused the decision by C-in-C and Naval Staff present, that it was no longer realistic to make *Tirpitz* ready for sea, or action again. Decision was made to move *Tirpitz* to a shallow berth near Tromsø where she could not be sunk and would be used as a floating battery.

15 October 1944: After temporary repairs, *Tirpitz* was transferred from Kaafjord to Sørbotn off the island of Håkøya near Tromsø, Norway. The ship was only able to make 10 knots during this short voyage.

16 October 1944: Arrived at Sørbotn. The sea bed below the ship was sandy and there was only 1.5 meters of water between the ship's keel and the sea bed.

29 October 1944: Operation Obviate, *Tirpitz* was attacked with "Tall Boy" bombs by 39 Lancasters (19 Lancasters of 617 Squadron and 20 Lancasters of 9 Squadron). Only one near miss was scored, which exploded about 15 m off the port side in the region of the steering gear. The damage was severe, but inconsequen-

tial.

12 November 1944: Operation Catechism, 31 British Lancaster bombers from 9 and 617 Squadrons attacked *Tirpitz* with "Tall Boy" bombs. After three hits and several near misses the battleship capsized to port at 0952 hrs. It is unclear how many crew were actually on board when the ship was sunk. But of the approximately 1700-1900 men on board, 971 were lost. Among those were the ships captain, Robert Weber and most of the officers. 87 crew members were rescued by cutting holes in the ship's bottom to compartments where they had climbed. The British bombers suffered no losses.

1948-1957: The wreck of the Tirpitz was broken up and sold as scrap by the Norwegian company Einar Høvding Skippsuphugging which bought the wreck from the Norwegian government. Einar Høvding Skippsuphugging paid 120,000 Norwegian kroner for the wreck in 1948.

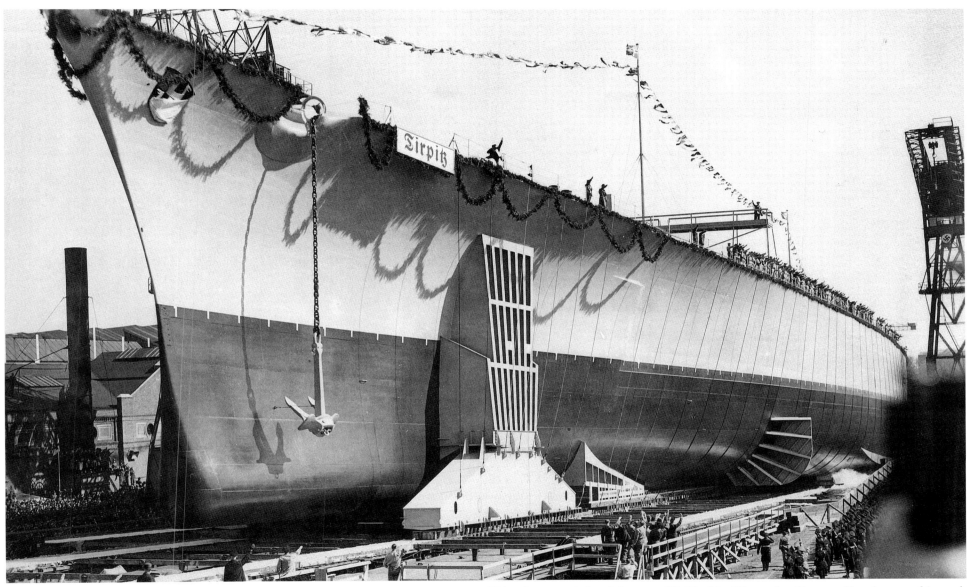

This photograph is of the new "Battleship G", at the German Navy's own shipyard, Kriegsmarine Werft, in Wilhelmshaven. The new ship was christened by Frau von Hassel and named Tirpitz, *after her father Grand Admiral Alfred von Tirpitz. The launch took place on April 1st, 1939 in the presence of Adolf Hitler and a large number of personalities from the navy, politicians, business and industry leaders, together with a crowd of about 80,000 people.*

Tirpitz *in the photos on this page is shown with a special camouflage to make the warship look like the surrounding buildings while in the 40,000 ton floating dock. The photograph was taken in Wilhelmshaven in 1940 during the fitting-out period.*

This photograph was taken in late 1940 at the naval shipyard in Wilhelmshaven. Tirpitz was near completion and painted in a camouflage pattern representing the barracks. Numerous times, the British RAF tried to bomb Tirpitz and other German warships in Wilhelmshaven. In fact the first attack on German territory in WWII took place September 4th, 1939, when RAF tried to bomb the German ships in Wilhelmshaven.

This photograph, taken in the winter of 1940, showing Tirpitz near completion. This starboard portrait of the fore half of the ship shows many details like the funnel construction and bridge tower. Some of the small boats have already been installed, likewise the searchlights, AA artillery director and the fore and middle 150 mm secondary turrets. This photograph also documents that the local rangefinders on the "Anton," or "A," forward main turret were installed. They were removed before the ship was commissioned February 25th., 1941 based on experiences from sistership Bismarck. Salt water coming in over the forecastle entered the rangefinders and caused problems and malfunctioning. It was therefore decided to remove the local rangefinders on this main turret on both ships.

Tirpitz *arriving in Gotenhafen in the spring of 1941 to carry out trials in the Baltic Sea. At this point the 10.5 m and 7 m rangefinders, as well as the FuMO23 radar have yet to be installed. Also, the two aft AA 4 m type SL-8 rangefinders were still missing their protective cupola at the time of this image being taken.*

The photograph in the lower left corner shows Tirpitz *during the sea trial period in summer 1941 with an assisting tug on her starboard side.*

A summer 1941 close-up view of the two aft main turrets, "Caesar" and "Dora." The ship's officers are lined up for group photos to be taken.

Another photograph showing Tirpitz during her working up period in the Baltic Sea. At this time of the war the Baltic Sea was a safe area for German warships to carry out sea trials as it was outside the range of British bomber aircraft. The 10.5 m rangefinder and the FuMO23 radar were installed at the time of this photograph on the conning tower and the foretop, although it has yet to be installed on the aft fire control center.

Another spring 1941 portrait of Tirpitz. *When German warships were commissioned they were painted with a light grey superstructure and medium grey hull.* Tirpitz *wore these so-called peacetime colors until July 1941 when the turret tops were painted black.*

A photograph illustrating the power and strength of Tirpitz *with all his main guns raised and steaming at high speed during gunnery practice in the summer of 1941. The main turret tops were painted black. The superstructure was still painted light grey and the hull medium grey.*

Two photographs showing Tirpitz *during gunnery practice in the Baltic Sea during the summer of 1941. As on other German warships, the main turrets were called A (Anton), B (Bruno), C (Caesar) and D (Dora) from fore to aft.*

The smaller photograph to the right shows Tirpitz *firing a full salvo from both forward main turrets.*

The photographs on this and the next page show Tirpitz *during gunnery practice in the summer of 1941. The rings of metal around the barrels of the main guns and the covers on the barrels on the C turret was a heat-protection system meant to avoid one-sided cooling and heating of the barrels. This was done in order to minimize the ballistic influences that could have affected the accuracy of the shot. The Germans experimented with this system on both* Bismarck *and* Tirpitz. *Ironically, their biggest problem was the quality of the ammunition, as many rounds fired by* Bismarck *at* Hood *and* Prince of Wales *failed to explode.*

The two photographs on this page were taken during the June-July 1941 period. The upper image was during his gunnery trials, while the lower image shows Tirpitz *slowly passing a small sailing vessel in the Baltic Sea.*

These two images date from sometime during the 1941 sea trials in the Baltic Sea.

The smaller photo above is of a few of the crew conferring in front of one of the twin 105 mm Flak mounts.

The larger image was taken from the main deck amidships, looking up and forward, towards the bridge.

Two more photographs from the sea trial period in 1941. Like many other German warships, Tirpitz was known to be rather wet on the fore part of the ship, as seen in the portrait to the left. The main photograph on this page shows the port boat and aircraft crane, one of the 105 mm heavy AA guns and also the portside middle 150 mm secondary turret, with its 6.5 m local rangefinder.

In the summer of 1941, the Germans made a propaganda film of Tirpitz with the help of one of the ships own Arado Ar196A aircraft. Main turret A is trained to port and the details on the superstructure are clearly visible. Based on experiences with Bismarck it was decided to slightly rearrange the midship section. The boat and aircraft cranes were placed one deck higher than on Bismarck as seen in the photograph below. The superstructure in this area was built out to accommodate this modification. The seaplane was painted green (see pages 36 & 37 for details).

Another photograph from the time of the propaganda filming. The Arado Ar196A floatplane from the Tirpitz landed on the water after the filming to be lifted back on board.

Portside view of Tirpitz in the summer of 1941. The ship was still not fully equipped. The aft 10.5 m rangefinder and FuMO23 radar were still missing at that time, as well as the cupola for the two aft 4 m Type SL-8 rangefinders used to direct the lighter AA guns.

Two detail photographs of the aft portion of Tirpitz *, taken during June-July 1941, while on trials in the Baltic Sea. The after rangefinder and AA directors have yet to be installed at the date of these images. There is, however a temporary 4 m rangefinder fitted atop the aft fire control station during this time, visible in the image above.*

The photographs on the previous page were taken on May 5th, 1941, when Adolf Hitler visited Tirpitz *in Gotenhafen. In company with Admiral Günther Lütjens and other German military personnel, Hitler was given a tour around the newest German battle-ship by its captain, Friedrich Carl Topp.*

The photo on this page was taken at the commissioning ceremony February 25th, 1940, in Wilhelmshaven.

After the loss of Bismarck on May 27th, 1941, the German Naval Command was afraid of losing the sistership Tirpitz in the same manner. The Germans attacked the Soviet Union on June 22nd, 1941 and as of August 1941, American and British convoys started to supply the Soviet Union with military equipment and supplies to help fight the Germans. Based on this, the German Naval Command decided to change their strategy. Tirpitz was transferred to Norway to be a threat to the Allied convoys and to force the British to use a significant number of warships to protect these convoys. This photo shows Tirpitz in the winter of 1942 shortly after arrival to Norway. Notice the Arado floatplane flying in the background carrying out reconnaissance.

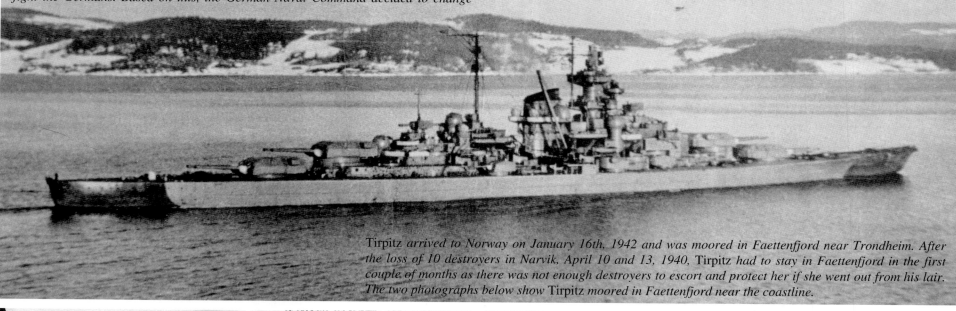

Tirpitz arrived to Norway on January 16th, 1942 and was moored in Faettenfjord near Trondheim. After the loss of 10 destroyers in Narvik, April 10 and 13, 1940, Tirpitz had to stay in Faettenfjord in the first couple of months as there was not enough destroyers to escort and protect her if she went out from his lair. The two photographs below show Tirpitz moored in Faettenfjord near the coastline.

24

This photograph was taken by a British reconnaissance aircraft and shows Tirpitz *in Faettenfjord in early summer 1942. Notice the two newly installed quadruple 20 mm AA guns mounted in front of the open bridge and on top of the B main turret.*

The two photographs below were taken March 9th, 1942, during Operation "Sportpalast", Tirpitz *first attempt to attack Allied convoys. Due to bad weather she was unable to locate the convoys PQ12 and QP8. When* Tirpitz *was on its way back to Faettenfjord she was attacked by 12 Albacores from aircraft carrier* H.M.S. Victorious.

Tirpitz *avoided all torpedoes by making evasive maneuvers and managed to shoot down two Albacores with its anti-aircraft guns. This photograph was taken during that torpedo attack.*

This photograph shows Tirpitz *on her way to Bogen near Narvik. It was decided to seek refuge there instead of going directly back to Faettenfjord.*

After the Albacore torpedo attack on March 9, 1942, Tirpitz anchored at Bogen and stayed there for three days before he went back to Faettenfjord near Trondheim. The unique photographs on this and the previous page show many details of the superstruc- *ture, weapons and radar. There was a lot of activity on board, with the manned AA weapons and the Arado aircraft on the catapult ready to be launched, reveals that the crew was prepared for a possible air attack from carrier aircraft.*

Two more detail photographs of Tirpitz taken at Bogen in March 1942. The left photograph shows that all the barrels of the 105 mm heavy AA guns are pointing up in the sky and the radar are turned to respectively port and starboard prepared for possible air attacks. On the photograph to the right, the single 20 mm light AA guns mounted just in front of the open bridge can be seen. In May 1942 they were replaced by two quadruple 20 mm guns placed in front of the bridge and on top of the B main turret.

The two photographs above and below were taken as the Tirpitz was launched, April 1st., 1939, Wilhelmshaven. At this time, the vessel is ridding very high in the water, but as the armor is added, superstructure is built up, weapons fitted, the ship will begin to approach it's massive 43,000+ tons.

The image to the right is of the aft deck and main gun turrets at sunset, somewhere in the Baltic Sea during trials in the summer of 1941.

This photograph shows Tirpitz *in Faettenfjord during the summer of 1942. A lot of effort was put into disguising the ship to make it look like the surrounding mountains by using, among other things, canvas and trees. The British mounted four air attacks and one attack by Chariots(manned torpedo) against* Tirpitz *in Faettenfjord in 1942. All attacks failed, despite the skills and bravery from the air crew and charioteers. Insufficient weapons and bad weather made it impossible to successfully attack the German battleship while it was in Faettenfjord.*

In July 1942 Tirpitz made it's second and last attempt to attack Allied convoys to and from the Soviet Union. The convoy, PQ17, was the biggest convoy so far carrying military equipment worth $700 million. The Germans prepared an attack with Tirpitz and other surface units, transferring Tirpitz from Faettenfjord, via Bogen, to Altafjord in northern Norway. With that maneuver, Tirpitz disappeared from British reconnaissance and was believed to be en route to attack the convoy. PQ17 and its escorting warships were told to scatter in an effort to disperse and evade the German naval force. The unprotected merchant ships were slaughtered by German U-boats and Luftwaffe aircraft. Tirpitz, heavy cruisers Admiral Hipper and Admiral Scheer, and six escorting destroyers departed Norway on July 5th., 1942, to assist in attacking the convoy, but successful attacks by U-boats and aircraft made it unnecessary to risk Tirpitz and she and her task force were called back to base a few hours later.

The upper photograph on the previous page was taken July 5th., from destroyer Z6 Theodor Riedel, as the German task force arrived back to Norway.

The lower photograph on the previous page was most likely taken during Operation "Rösselsprung."

The image to the right is of the Tirpitz under tow in the Faettenfjord sometime during the summer of 1942. This photograph was taken from the tugboat Arngast.

The photograph below is an aerial view of Tirpitz, taken at Bogen, also during the summer of 1942. This image is actually a aerial reconnaissance photograph taken by the RAF.

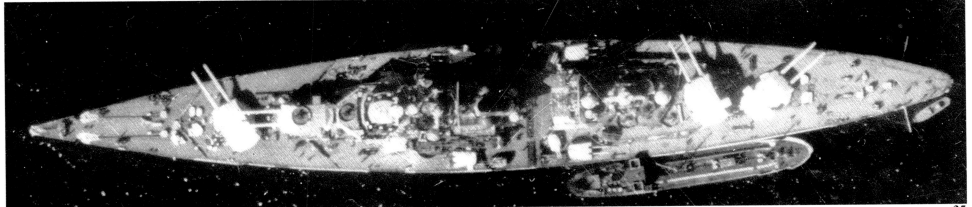

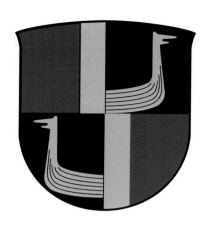

KM TIRPITZ
MARCH - JULY 1944

Port Side

Starboard Side

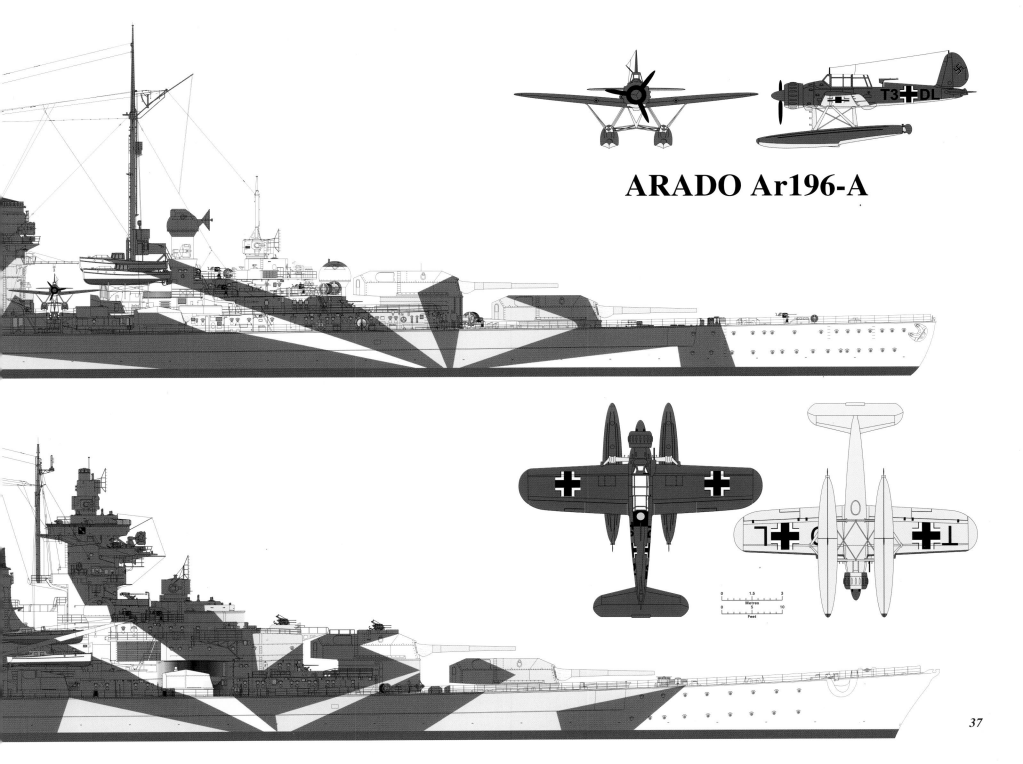

ARADO Ar196-A

Two photographs of Tirpitz in Bogen, near Narvik, in the summer of 1942. Narvik was a vital port for Germany, as iron ore mined in Sweden was transported by rail to Narvik and from there, shipped to Germany. Narvik was one of the biggest German naval bases in Norway during the Second World War.

In the large photograph on this page, a mountain can be seen behind Tirpitz's B main turret, that the crew nicknamed "The Elephant" because of its shape.

KM TIRPITZ

June - July 1942
Port

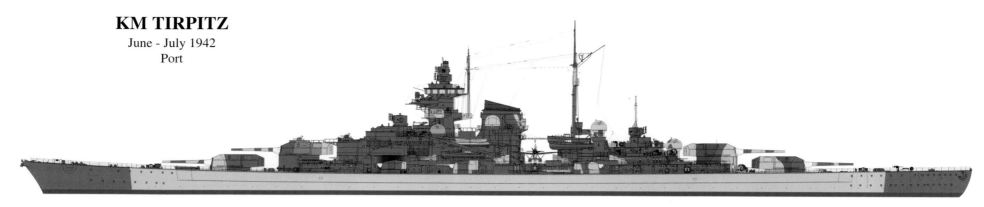

Tirpitz at anchor in the Farttenfjord, about June 1942. This is the only known color photograph of this camouflage pattern to hide this battleship against the shoreline in Norway.

KM TIRPITZ

June - July 1942
Starboard

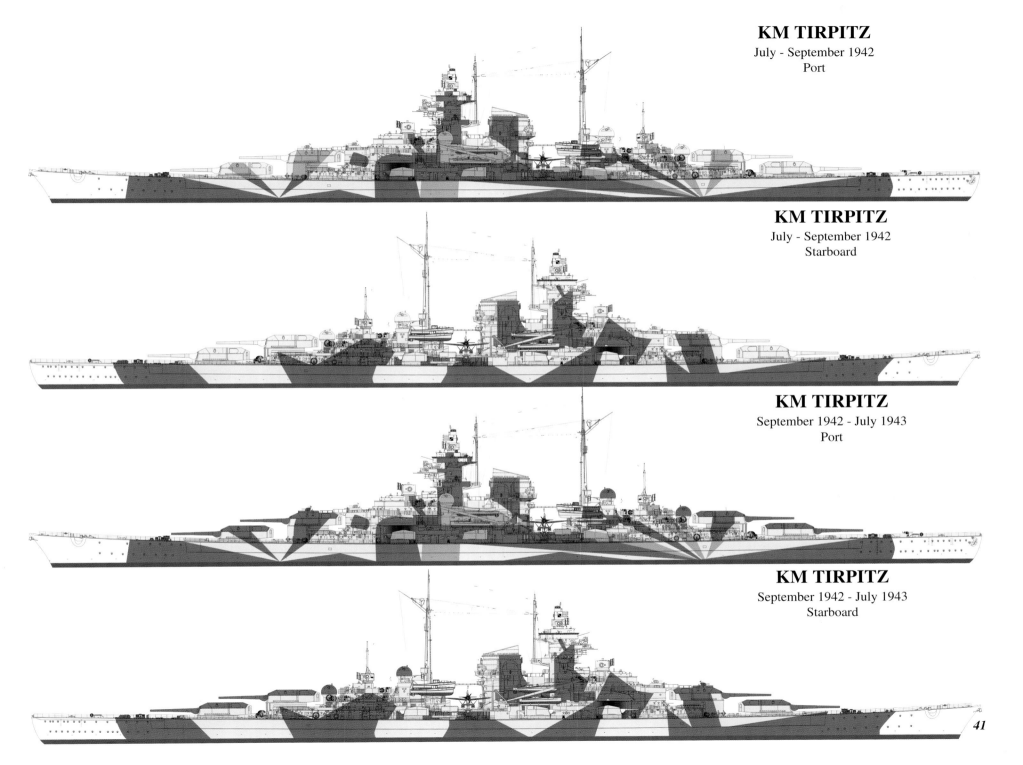

KM TIRPITZ
July - September 1942
Port

KM TIRPITZ
July - September 1942
Starboard

KM TIRPITZ
September 1942 - July 1943
Port

KM TIRPITZ
September 1942 - July 1943
Starboard

41

The photographs on this page were all possibly taken during Operation "Rösselsprung," July 5th., 1942.

The photograph on the left was taken on July 5th., 1942, during Operation "Rösselsprung." Following Tirpitz *were the torpedo boats T7 and T15, and the heavy cruiser* Admiral Hipper. *This image was taken from the back of the bridge, looking aft.*

A view of the mainmast on Tirpitz *from the main deck aft, taken in Faettenfjord, summer of 1942.*

KM TIRPITZ

July 1943 - March 1944
Port

KM TIRPITZ

July 1943 - March 1944
Starboard

Tirptiz *off of Spitsbergen, just after the conclusion of the bombardment of that Allied facility, September 1943.*

KM TIRPITZ

July - November 1944
Port

The photograph at left, top, was taken at Bogen. The remainder of the images are of some of the small boats carried aboard the Tirpitz. The image below was taken aft of the aft boat mooring boom, looking forward, also taken at Bogen. The middle left image is of one of the motor launches, while the lower left image is of members of the crew in a launch practicing rowing.

The heavy cruiser Admiral Scheer *at Bogen during the summer of 1942, as seen look-ing over the foredeck of the* Tirpitz. *The* Lützow (*ex-*Deutschland) *and the* Admiral Scheer *were re-rated from "Panzerschiff," or armored ships, to heavy cruisers about 1941. Note the floats for the anti-torpedo net forward of the bow of* Tirpitz.

Tirpitz, Admiral Hipper, Admiral Scheer *and escort leaving Altafjord to assist in attacking convoy PQ17, July 5th, 1942 during Operation "Rösselsprung." That operation was cancelled four hours later. This photograph was taken from destroyer Z-28.*

This photograph shows Tirpitz *and* Lützow *(far left) in Kaafjord, near Alta, in April 1943.* Tirpitz *was transferred to Kaafjord in March 1943 and stayed there for the next year. In Kaafjord,* Tirpitz *was outside the range of RAF land based aircraft stationed in the UK and also closer to the Arctic convoy routes.*

Two photographs from April and later in the summer of 1943 of Tirpitz in Kaafjord. In both photographs the 105 mm heavy AA gun barrels are raised ready to be used in case of air attacks. Notice the Swastika on the aft part of the main deck to reduce the risk of attacks from German aircraft (friendly fire).

The photograph at left on the previous page is of the bridge tower of Tirpitz while at Faettenfjord, Norway, June-July 1942. The director and rangefinder atop the bridge were facing aft. The image on the right of the previous page is of the backside of the funnel, as seen from aft. Around it was a platform to hold searchlights and light anti-aircraft guns.

Both of the photographs on this page are of the Tirpitz while at Kaafjord, Norway, taken about July 1943 through March 1944. Both the port and starboard sides of the camouflage pattern are visible in these images.

This is one of very few on board views of Tirpitz during his career. This photograph was taken about August through September 1943. As can be seen by the lack of any visible wake, the ship is moving at a slow speed and is out to sea, another rare event for that warship. Take a close look at the foredeck planking and the fashion in which it was laid out. Also note the swastika painted on the deck for recognition purposes. It was painted on a red background.

This is a view from the stern deck aboard the Tirpitz during the same voyage as the photograph from the previous page. These images may be when the battleship was approaching Altafjord, Norway. The wood decking appears rather dark, which leads us to believe that the deck may have been painted at that time. The color may have been a dark gray, or even a dark gray/blue. Note the single 20 mm AA mounts on the stern deck, as well as all those on the superstructure have their barrels pointed skyward in anticipation of an air attack.

A starboard amidship view of the two 105 mm heavy anti-aircraft guns in twin mountings and the center 150 mm turret. Note the different grey camouflage patterns applied to the gun barrels. To the right is a pinnace (boat) with the admiral's pennant on the bow.

A view over Tirpitz's *forecastle, taken in Bogen, near Narvik in 1942. The two quadruple 20 mm light anti-aircraft guns (flakvierling) mounted in front of the open bridge and on top of the B main turret were covered with canvas for protection against weather. The crew were on parade by division.* Tirpitz's *crew was divided into twelve divisions as follows: Division 1-4 - seaman branch including personnel for the main and secondary armament; Division 5-6 - seaman branch including flak personnel; Division 7 - functionaries; Division 8 - artillery mechanical personnel; Division 9 - navigation and signals; Division 10-12 - ships technicians.*

All of the photographs from both this and the previous page are from the attack by the German Navy upon Spitsbergen, September 8th, 1943. Spitsbergen is a large island group about 500 miles north of the northern most point of Norway, very close to the North Pole. This is above the Barents Sea, on the edge of the Arctic Ocean. This location was used by the Allies as a meteorological station to assist the convoys traveling to and from Murmansk, Russia (Soviet Union). The German Naval task force consisted of the battleships Tirpitz and Scharnhorst, along with nine destroyers as escort. They bombarded and destroyed the Allied base and returned to Kaafjord and Langfjord, Norway. The two top images on the previous page were taken on board Tirpitz, while the rest of the photographs on this and the previous page were all taken from the destroyer Z-10 Hans Lody. Note the camouflage pattern on the Scharnhorst in the main photograph on this page.

One of the Arado Ar196A floatplanes being hoisted on board Tirpitz, on the battleship's port side by the huge boat and aircraft crane. In the background the destroyer Z14 Friedrich Ihn can be seen. That destroyer would be one of the few that survived the entire war, taken by the Soviet Union as part of war reparations in late 1945.

Images on this page are of the battleship's aircraft type, the Arado Ar196A. The two top images are of 100th. launching of a floatplane from the Tirpitz's catapult. Although the two lower images show a portion of the catapult, these photos are really of the X-Craft attack on September 22nd, 1943. Tirpitz's guns shoot against X-5, a British midget submarine. For more information on this event, see the history section on page 3.

This aerial view is a reconnaissance photograph taken of the Tirpitz *in Kaafjord after the X-craft attack in September 1943. The crippled battleship is leaking oil from the fuel tanks. Note the camouflage pattern on the deck.*

The image above is of the Tirpitz *and an escorting destroyer taken during his working up period after repairs from damage caused by British X-craft.*

This photograph and the two lower images on the previous page are of Tirpitz taken during sea trials in Altafjord in spring 1944. The battleship had just completed damage repairs from the British X-craft raid in September 1943. The Würzburg radar was now present just behind the main mast, mounted onto the dome of the AA director.

This is an aerial photograph taken by attacking British Royal Navy carrier based bombers during an April 3rd., 1944 attack. Tirpitz was hit by 15 bombs, with severe damage and a high loss of crewmen, 120 killed and 316 wounded.

Tirpitz under repair after the April 3rd, 1944 British carrier based air attack. That attack caused serious damage to the German battleship that required technicians from Germany to travel to Norway to repair the warship.

This photograph, looking aft from the back of the bridge tower, shows some of the extensive damage caused by the British carrier based Barracuda attack bombers. In the foreground is what is left of the port searchlight position after a direct hit. At least 14 bombs hit the Tirpitz, with four near misses also causing damage. The British aircraft were carrying either three 500 lb., or one 1,600 lb. bombs per plane. The results of this raid were demoralizing for the crew of this German Battleship.

All of the images on this page are of the damage caused by the air attack of April 3rd., 1944. Since the British attack did not encounter any German fighter cover, the escorting Corsair, Hellcat and Wildcat fighters strafed the Tirpitz one after another, prior to

the Barracuda bombers attack. Many of the anti-aircraft and director crews were slaughtered by this. The bomb hits made matters worse, as the German crew struggled to establish any sort of damage control.

The two photographs on this page show Tirpitz *in her final camouflage scheme in the summer of 1944 during sea trials in Altafjord. That would be the last time that the giant battleship would put out to sea. He operated with the destroyers Z-29, Z-31, Z-33, Z-34, and Z-39. These images are of what is believed to be the last camouflage pattern worn* by this ship. The colors may have been as follows: Hull - Dunkelgrau 2 (a very dark gray, almost light black), Superstructure - Dunkelgrau (normally the standard hull color), Bridge Top - Weiss (white).

Both of the photographs on this page are of the sinking of Tirpitz, taken on November 12th, 1944, by a German crew member from one of the anti-aircraft battery locations. Tirpitz received 3 direct hits by "Tall Boy" bombs and capsized to port. These bombs weighed in at a colossal 12,000 lbs., or 6 tons each. Little did the British know, but the Tirpitz had already been rendered inoperable by a previous raid with "Tall Boys" back on September 15th., 1944. Two of these bombs hit the bow and as repairs could not be rendered in Norway, the ship was to become a floating battery. So, had the British known this, this last raid would more than likely never have happened. The official number of casualties aboard Tirpitz was 971 German sailors, nearly half the entire crew.

After the Tirpitz *capsized, the Germans immediately tried to rescue sailors trapped inside the ship by cutting holes in the hull. They managed to rescue 87 sailors this way. These two photographs show this rescue attempt underway. The Germans salvaged some vital parts from* Tirpitz *before the end of the war. Among other things, the ship's* propellers. *The photograph in the lower right corner shows two Germans inspecting the starboard shaft and propeller mounting. The propeller has already been removed when the photograph was taken.*

The three photographs on this page were taken after the war showing the scrapping of the Tirpitz.

The top photograph is of the wreck being broken up, about 1950. The steel was sold as scrap by the Norwegian company Einar Høvding Skippsuphugging which bought the wreck from the Norwegian government in 1948 paying 120,000 Norwegian kroner for the wreck. Scrapping was finished about 1957.

The photograph in the lower left corner shows the salvage of one of the ships 150 mm secondary turrets.

The photograph in the lower right corner shows the salvage of the ships B main turret.

Parts of the battleship still remain on the bottom of this shallow part of Sørbotn off the island of Håkøya near Tromsø, Norway, and most recently, one of the Arado aircraft was also discovered nearby.

General Statistics of the German Battleship Tirpitz

Dimensions (ft.)

length overall................................831.8 (253.6 m)
beam...118 (36 m)
draught   (min.).................32.47 (9.9 m)
               (max.)..............34.77 (10.6 m)

Displacement (metric tons)

standard..43,344
full-load..49,947
battle-load..50,954

Propulsion

boilers.............................12 Wagner small tube
engines..........3 sets Brown, Boveri & Cie geared turbines
propellers...3 manganese bronze 3 blade, diameter 15.5ft.
top speed...30.80 kts.
shaft horsepower designed...................................138,000
               1941 trials................................163,026
fuel capacity   1941............................8,297 metric tons

Endurance

1941..................................4,728 nm. @ 28 kts.
                   6,963 nm. @ 24 kts.
                   8,870 nm. @ 19 kts.

Aircraft

Arado Ar-196-A...4
Individual aircraft identification numbers BB+YF,
T3+BL, T3+DL, T3+GK, T3+HK, T3+LH, & T3+LK

Complement

1941...103 officers & 1,976 men
1943...........................108 officers & approx. 2,500 men

Cost

1941................................191.6 million Reichs Mark

Armor (in.)

main belt	12.4 (315 mm), 5.7 (145-mm) upper, & 6.75 (170-mm) bottom.
	citadel............................5.75 (145 mm)
	outer skin: forward............2.4 (60 mm)
	aft................3.125 (80 mm)
	torpedo bulkhead.............1.75 (45 mm)
decks	forecastle......................1.125 (30 mm)
	upper................................2 (50 mm)
	main.............................3.125 (80 mm)
	over machinery............4.375 (110 mm)
	over magazine....................4 (100 mm)
	after..............................3.125 (80 mm)
	steering gear...............4.375 (110 mm)
bulkheads	8 (200 mm), 4 (100 mm), 3.125 (80 mm) & 1 (25 mm).
barbettes	13.375 (340 mm) forward, sides, 8.66 (220 mm) rear.
main turrets	14 (360 mm) face, 7 (180 mm) roof, 8.5 (220 mm) sides.

secondary turrets........4 (100 mm) face, 1.5 (40 mm) roof,
               sides & rear.
105 mm anti-aircraft mounts............ .75 (20 mm) shields
conning tower;
       forward 13.75 (350 mm) sides, 8 (200 mm) roof
       after 6 (150 mm) sides, 2 (50 mm) roof
main battery director/rangefinder;
       forward...............................4 (100 mm)
       foretop............................ .75 (20 mm)
       after...................................2 (50 mm)
anti-aircraft director/rangefinder.....................2 (50 mm)

anti-torpedo protection built into hull.

Armament

main...........8x15 in.(380 mm)/52 cal. in four twin turrets
secondary...12x5.9 in.(150 mm)/55 cal. in six twin turrets
AA armament: 4 in. (105 mm)/65 cal. twin mount......8
               37 mm/83 cal. twin mount..................8
               20 mm/65cal. quad mount(8/41)........6
               (6/44)................................18
               20 mm/65cal. single mount(2/41)......12
               (6/44)...............................6
torpedoes............ 2x21 in.(533 mm) deck mounted
quadruple mount. Installed summer 1941.

Ammunition

15 in. (380 mm)......................................840-960
5.9 in. (150 mm)......................................1800
4 in. (105 mm)..6,720
37 mm..32,000
20 mm................(8/41) 54,000.................(6/44) 117,000

Directors (ft.)

main turret rangefinders..............................34.5 (10.5 m)
       (removed from A turret in winter 1940/41)
midships secondary turret rangefinders.............21 (6.5 m)
main & secondary battery rangefinder/director;
       forward - w/FuMO 23 radar...................23 (7 m)
       foretop - w/FuMO 23 radar............34.5 (10.5 m)
       foretop - w/FuMO 27 radar
       after - w/FuMO 23 radar...............34.5 (10.5 m)
       (FuMO 23 and FuMO 27 replaced by FuMO 26
       during repairs, 10/43 - 3/44)
       fighting top - FuMB 4 SAMOS
       fore topmast - FuMO 30 Hohentwiel
       (installed 10/43 - 3/44)
anti-aircraft rangefinder/director;
       forward.........2 x 13 (4 m) Type SL8 bridge P&S
       after..2 x 13 (4 m) Type SL8 after superstructure

REFERENCES

Naval Radar
N. Friedman, Conway Maritime Press, 1988
Naval Weapons of WWII
J. Campbell, Conway Maritime Press, 1985
Zerstörer Unter Deutschen Flaggen 1934 bis 1945
W. Harnack, Koehlers Verlagsgesellschaft mbH, 1984
Tirpitz – Hunting the Beast
J. Sweetman, Sutton Publishing, 2000
Battleships–Axis and Neutral Battleships in World War II
W. Garzke & R. Dulin, Naval Institute Press, 1990
Battleships of the Bismarck Class
G. Koop & K.-P. Schmolke, Greenhill Books, 1998
Battleship Tirpitz
Siegfried Breyer, Schiffer Publishing Ltd, 1989
German Capital Ships of World War Two
M.J. Whitley, Arms & Armour, 2000

RESOURCES

W.A. Archibald, Pilot in RAF Bomber Command
http://mysite.wanadoo-members.co.uk/archie_bomber-command/index.html
Bismarck & Tirpitz Website
http://www.bismarck-class.dk
German Naval History
http://www.german-navy.de
Schlachtschiff Website
http://www.schlachtschiff.com
U. S. Naval Historical Center
Building 57, 805 Kidder Breese St. SE,
Washington Navy Yard, Washington DC, 20374-2571
(202)433-2765 • Web site: www.history.navy.mil
U. S. National Archives - Archives II
8601 Adelphi Rd., College Park, MD. 20740-6001
(301)713-6800 • Web site: www.nara.gov
U. S. Naval Institute
291 Wood Rd., Annapolis, MD 21402-5034
(800)233-8764 • Web site: www.usni.org

ACKNOWLEDGMENTS

Classic Warships
would like to express its gratitude to the following individuals
Don Montgomery • Steve Barker
Antonio Bonomi • Joachim Schaper
Even Blomkvist • Dirk Dühlmann-Valdeig
Linzee Druce • Markus Titsch • Wolfgang Harnack
Don Preul & Jeanne Pollard
Ed Finney, Rob Hanshew & Chuck Haberlein, Jr.
@ US Naval Historical Center
All the nice ladies on the 5th. floor @ Archives II

WARSHIP PICTORIAL SERIES

available at the time of this printing
W. P. # 4 USS Texas BB-35
W. P. # 7 New Orleans Class Cruisers
W. P. # 9 Yorktown Class Carriers
W. P. #10 Indianapolis & Portland
W. P. #12 Benson/Gleaves Class Destroyers
W. P. #14 USS Wichita CA-45
W. P. #17 IJN Myoko Class Cruisers
W. P. #18 USS New Mexico BB-40
W. P. #19 KM Bismarck
W. P. #20 HMS Hood
W. P. #22 USS Ticonderoga CV/CVA/CVS-14
W. P. #23 Italian Heavy Cruisers of WWII
W. P. #24 USN Areigh Burke Class Destroyers
W. P. #25 IJN Yamato Class Battleships
W. P. #26 KM Tirpitz
W. P. #27 KM Type VII U-boats

Front Cover: *Colorized black & white photograph of* Tirpitz *at anchor in Bogen, Norway, July 1942.*

Back Cover: *Collage of colorized black & white photographs to show* Tirpitz *steaming into one of the Norwegian Fjords.*

USS Arleigh Burke DDG-51, *a new class of destroyer for the United States Navy, is the subject of Warship Pictorial #24.*